Spies and Spying

WARTIME SPIES

Andrew Langley

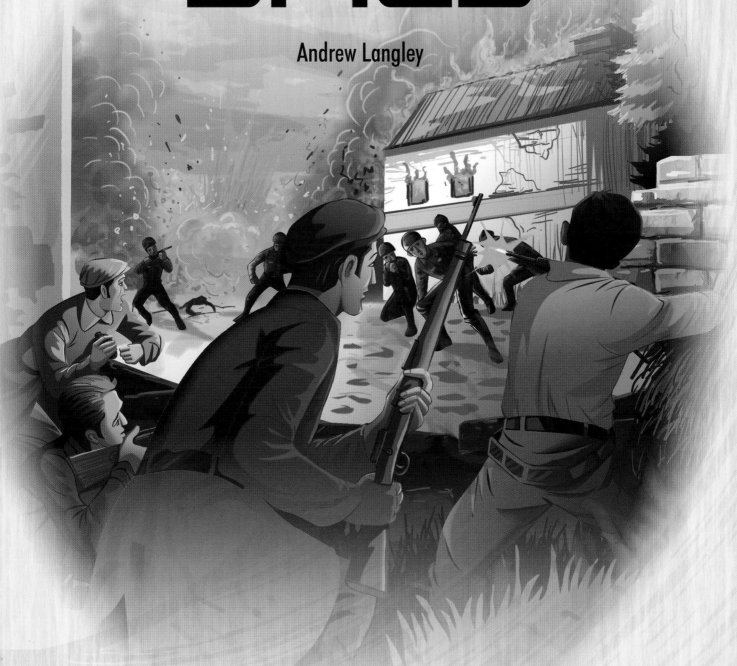

A+

Smart Apple Media

Smart Apple Media
P.O. Box 3263
Mankato, MN 56002

Printed in the United States of America

Library of Congress Cataloging-in-Publication Data

Langley, Andrew.
  Wartime spies / Andrew Langley.
     p. cm. -- (Spies and spying)
  Includes index.
  ISBN 978-1-59920-362-1 (hardcover)
  1. Spies--Juvenile literature. 2. Espionage--History--Juvenile literature. I. Title.
  UB270.5.L36 2010
  327.12--dc22
                          2008055505

Created by Q2AMedia
Editor: Jean Coppendale
Art Director: Rahul Dhiman
Designer: Ranjan Singh
Picture Researcher: Shreya Sharma
Line Artist: Sibi N. Devasia
Coloring Artists: Mahender Kumar, Aadil Ahmed siddiqui

All words in **bold** can be found in the glossary on pages 30–31.

Picture credits
t=top b=bottom
Cover image: Kiselev Andrey Valerevich/ Shutterstock, Inset: Q2AMedia: t, Q2AMedia: c, Q2AMedia: b,

Insides: Mark Goddard/ iStockphoto: 6, North Wind Picture Archives / Alamy: 8, Bibliothèque nationale de France: 9, Bob Thomas/
Popperfoto/ Contributor/ Getty Images: 11, Bettmann/ Corbis: 12, library of congress: 13t, Hulton Archive/ Stringer/ Getty Images: 15,
Library of congress: 17t, Library of Congress: 17b, The National Archive: 18, Mansell/ Stringer/ Time & Life Pictures/ Getty Images:
19b, Rex Features: 21, Associated Press: 22, Lockheed Martin: 25b, Federal Bureau of Investigation: 27t, Bettmann/ Corbis: 27b,
Dreamstime: 28, shutterstock: 29.

Q2AMedia Art Bank: Title Page, 4, 5, 7, 10, 13b, 14, 16, 19t, 20, 23, 24, 25t, 26, 31.

9 8 7 6 5 4 3 2 1

CONTENTS

SPYING ON THE ENEMY

People have been fighting wars and battles against enemy tribes and countries since history began. Spying has always been a vital part of warfare.

Know Your Enemy

The main job of a wartime spy is to find out as much information about the enemy as possible. How big is their army? What sort of weapons do they have? Do they have any weak points? What are their strengths? Wartime spying is about discovering information that the enemy wants to keep secret. Secret information that is valuable and reliable is called **intelligence**—it may help one side to win a war.

In wartime it is vital to find out where your enemy is positioned and if they plan to attack.

Behind the Lines

It is dangerous to be a spy at any time. But it is far more dangerous during wartime. To gather intelligence, spies have to go into enemy territory. They have to be very cunning to stay alive. They may also have to be masters of disguise, expert thieves, or ruthless killers. Some spies organize **resistance fighters** behind the enemy lines in order to carry out surprise attacks on soldiers or to **sabotage** important weapons or equipment.

During wartime, some spies help resistance fighters to sabotage enemy transportation networks.

Top Secret

In wartime, most countries follow the laws laid down by the **Geneva Convention**. These state that captured soldiers in uniform must be treated well. But spies may be in disguise, not in uniform. If they are caught by the enemy, they may be executed.

SPIES IN THE ANCIENT WORLD

Spies have been working behind enemy lines since warfare began. Their adventures have been recorded on clay tablets and **papyrus** rolls, and in books including the Bible.

Inside Information

War leaders of the ancient world knew the importance of intelligence. More than 3,500 years ago there was a spy inside the city of Babylon (in present-day Iraq). When the city was being **besieged**, he lit fires to show the enemy where to attack. The pharaohs of Egypt used a system of spies (usually merchants) to send news from other lands. This gave them early warning of any invasion or revolt.

The Ancient Egyptians sometimes used hieroglyphics (picture writing) to send messages.

Tricked!

In 218 B.C., the African leader Hannibal marched his army—and a herd of elephants—through the Alps into Italy. At first, he won battles against the Romans. But the Roman general, Scipio, captured some of Hannibal's spies, showed them his camp and let them go. The spies reported to Hannibal that Scipio was short of cavalry, so Hannibal decided to attack. But a large Roman cavalry was arriving the next day. When the two sides met in battle, the Romans won.

Both Hannibal and his enemies in Ancient Rome used spies in their wars against each other.

SPY FILE

Demaratus c.480 B.C.

Demaratus was an ex-Greek king living in Persia (modern Iran). King Xerxes of Persia planned to send a surprise naval force to invade Greece. Demaratus knew he had to warn the Greeks, so he sent them hidden messages on wax-covered tablets. They were blank on the outside but when the wax was scraped off the messages were written in the wood underneath. When the Persian fleet arrived, the Greeks were waiting!

THE FIRST SPYMASTERS

Behind every system or network of secret agents is the spymaster. He or she is the brains of the network and organizes and controls everything. The earliest spymasters were also military leaders.

Spies Are Everywhere

The Muslim leader Saladin (c. 1138–93) made clever use of spies to defeat the invading Crusader armies.

Nine centuries ago, Europe's Crusader armies occupied parts of the Middle East. But the Muslims had a new leader, Salah ad-Din (Saladin) who was determined to drive them out. Saladin built up a vast network of spies. They could move easily among the Arab crowds and not be spotted by the Crusader guards. Saladin's spies gave him vital intelligence that helped him to defeat the Crusaders in crucial battles.

Captain Firouz

In 1098, Crusaders besieged the city of Antioch. Firouz, a Muslim army officer and spy, was in command of one of the towers in the city wall. He sent a message to the Crusaders to bring ladders to the tower at nightfall. When they climbed up, he let them in through a window. The secret attack worked, and soon Antioch was in Christian hands.

SPY FILE

The Horns of Hattin

The turning point for the Crusades came in 1187. A vast Crusader army was marching to attack Saladin's troops at Tiberias (in present-day Israel). Their route lay through roasting desert, and Saladin's spies told him that the invaders had no water carts. He knew they would run out of water and head for the nearest springs, at the Horns of Hattin. Saladin waited for the exhausted enemy to arrive, then attacked. His great victory shattered the entire Crusading movement.

This medieval painting shows the siege of Antioch. The city of Antioch fell into the hands of the Crusaders in 1098 as a result of the treachery of Firouz, a captain of the guard within the city.

Top Secret

What happens when you don't use spies?

October 25, 1415: Agincourt, France

French forces: 25,000   English forces: 6,000

French spywork: none (they thought they were bound to win)

What didn't they know about? A new English weapon, the longbow, which shot arrows quicker, further, and harder than the French crossbow.

What happened? The English won an amazing victory—thanks to the longbow.

Terror from the East

Genghis Khan (1162–1227) was the most terrifying conqueror the world had ever seen. In the early 1200s, his **Mongol** armies swept across Asia from China to Persia. City after city fell before them. But this was not just because they were fearsome fighters. Genghis Khan sent spies to the towns ahead of his army. They scared people by telling them the Mongols were coming, and told them they had a choice. They could fight and be massacred, or they could surrender and be spared. No wonder many towns gave up without a fight.

Genghis Khan sent spies in front of his armies to spread terror stories among enemy forces.

The Cardinal and the Cabinet Noir

Cardinal Richelieu was France's first spymaster. During the Thirty Years' War (1618–48), between Protestants and Catholics in Europe, he claimed to have spies in every court and city in Europe. His closest agents formed a top secret service called the Cabinet Noir (Black Cabinet), steaming open every letter that moved through France, and bribing or torturing suspects. In 1635, France declared war on Spain. Thanks to his Black Cabinet, Richelieu discovered that the French Queen was sending secret messages to the Spanish king (her brother).

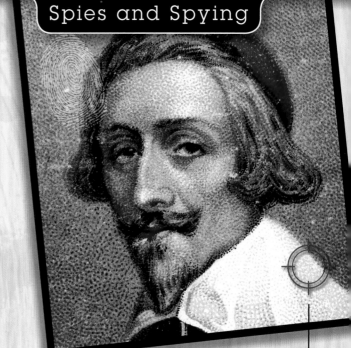

Cardinal Richelieu (1585-1642) was chief minister to King Louis XIII of France. Richelieu set up an intelligence service called the Cabinet Noir. His spies helped prevent plots against the king.

Top Secret

How Richelieu's men got information out of an enemy agent:

1. Caught him.
2. Tied his hands to one end of the rack, and his ankles to the other.
3. Turned the handles so that his body was stretched.
4. Waited for him to spill the beans.

SPY FILE

Francois de Tremblay

(1577–1638)

Tremblay was one of Richelieu's most valuable agents. Known as the l'Eminence Grise (Gray Eminence) because of the gray monk's habit that he wore, he set up an extensive spy system among Catholic monks in Europe. His undercover work and **bribery** helped cause the murder of a key Austrian general.

SPYING FOR THE REVOLUTION

Well-trained spies can make all the difference between winning and losing a war.

A Bad Start

During the **American Revolution** (1775–83), the English had only untrained spies who gathered scraps of intelligence. They claimed that the American rebels were weak and badly organized. Full of confidence, an English force marched to seize the arms depot in Concord, Massachusetts. When their way was blocked by American fighters, the English opened fire—expecting the opposition to run away. But the Americans fired back, forcing the English to hasty retreat.

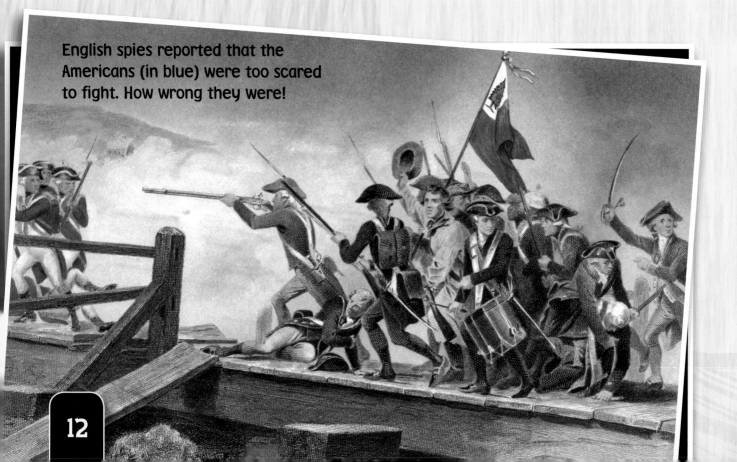

English spies reported that the Americans (in blue) were too scared to fight. How wrong they were!

Outwitting the English

The Culper Ring was a chain of secret agents set up by **George Washington**, the leader of the American forces. It brought intelligence from English-held New York back to Washington's headquarters in New Jersey. It also fed false information to the enemy. In 1781, the English received reports that the Americans were about to attack New York, so they rushed troops to defend it. But the report was a colonial trick. The American army was actually going to Yorktown, where it secured a crucial victory.

George Washington crosses the Delaware River for his surprise attack on Yorktown.

Top Secret

Anna Smith Strong was the only female member of the Culper Ring. She had an unusual signal to tell American agents that there was a ship waiting to pick up intelligence reports:

1. Watch for the ship to arrive off the coast.
2. Hang out a black petticoat on the clothes line to alert agents.
3. Also hang out a number of handkerchiefs, to indicate the ship's exact location.

Watching the Enemy

Napoleon Bonaparte, leader of France (1799–1815), planned to invade Britain but first he had to defeat the British Royal Navy. British spies wandered around foreign ports, counting French ships and troops and copying French dispatches. This meant that the British naval commander, Admiral Nelson, knew just what the French fleet was up to, and he won a brilliant victory over the French at Trafalgar in 1805.

Napoleon invaded Russia in 1812 without sending spies ahead of his army. The result was a disaster.

14

Napoleon: Spyless in Russia

Napoleon suffered his worst military disaster through lack of information from his spies. In June 1812, he led a vast French army to invade Russia, without a proper spy system to warn him of the dangers ahead. So he did not know about the Russian army's tactics (refusing to fight a **pitched battle**). He also did not know that Moscow would be deserted and stripped of all food and supplies. Then, when he finally made the decision to retreat, his troops were not prepared for the hellish conditions of the Russian winter.

SPY FILE

Charles Schulmeister

(1770–1853)

During the Napoleonic Wars, Schulmeister became one of the most powerful spies in history. He became the intelligence chief of the Austrian army—while actually working for the French! Schulmeister fed fake information to the Austrians. In 1805, this led them into a fatal trap at the Battle of Ulm, which seriously weakened France's enemies.

Top Secret

The British Post Office had a vital—secret—part to play in the wars against Napoleon. Its operatives opened and read all letters leaving or entering the country. This turned up many juicy bits of valuable intelligence.

AGENTS FOR THE UNION

The American Civil War (1861–65) was a bitter conflict. One of the reasons why the **Union** won was that they used spies more cleverly—though not always.

A Lost Opportunity

In 1862, the Union army was ready to fight the **Confederacy**. But Allan Pinkerton, head of the Union spy network, warned that the Confederates had over 150,000 men. The attack was delayed and the opportunity lost. Pinkerton's intelligence turned out to be wrong—the enemy had only 50,000 men. Pinkerton resigned soon afterwards.

Allan Pinkerton rode as a guard behind Abraham Lincoln's carriage when Lincoln was declared U.S. president in 1861.

From Slavery to Spying

The Union in the U.S. Civil War was rarely short of **volunteer** spies. Many people were eager to help defeat the Confederacy, which represented southern slave owners. The Union's new spymaster, George H. Sharpe, **recruited** hundreds of runaway slaves, who could easily **infiltrate** Confederate areas. Sharpe also employed many female agents. He realized that women were less likely to be suspected of spying than men.

This telegraph station was used in the American Civil War. Many of the operators were civilians who helped with vital communication and with the coordination of troop movements over vast distances.

Sarah Emma Edmonds

(1841–98)

Sarah Edmonds fought for the Union army—as a male soldier called Franklin T. Thompson. Then (still as a man) she was chosen to be a spy. She traveled behind Confederate lines in several disguises, once as a black man called Ned, and once as an Irish pedlar called Bridget.

Top Secret

The American Civil War showed the importance of the new electric telegraph system. Messages could be sent immediately over long distances. But they could also be **intercepted** by the enemy. The Unionists soon cracked the code used by the Confederacy.

THE GREAT WAR

By the time World War I (1914–18) began, the development of radio had made sending long-distance messages easier—but more **vulnerable**.

Cracking the German Code

Early in the war, the **Allies** captured a German naval code book, which allowed them to read important messages. But in 1915, a German team began writing a new code book. One member was Alexander Szek, whose parents lived in England. A British agent in Berlin contacted Szek and threatened to send his family to prison if he did not hand over the new code. Szek agreed, and smuggled out the code book on tiny scraps of paper. When the job was over, British agents had murdered Szek anyway.

Radio operators work among ruined buildings during World War I. The invention of radio allowed soldiers to send and receive messages instantly on the battlefield.

Carl Hans Lody (1877–1914)

In July 1914, German Carl Hans Lody began spying on British naval movements in the Edinburgh docks. His reports led to the sinking of a British warship by a German **U-boat.** But Lody was soon arrested and executed by a firing squad in the Tower of London—just a few weeks into the war.

SPY FILE

School for Spies

Elsbeth Schragmüller, known simply as "Fraulein Doktor" (Miss Doctor) was a brilliant intelligence chief. She set up her spy school in Antwerp, Belgium, in 1914. First-time secret agents were given special training. Students spent 15 weeks learning spy skills, such as using invisible ink and working undercover. The students wore masks so that they would never recognize (or betray) each other in the field.

Pigeons were used to carry vital messages across war-torn Europe. But they had to make a dangerous double journey. In England, the birds were carefully strapped into a wicker basket. The basket was then flown by aircraft behind enemy lines and dropped by parachute to the waiting agents. The agents put their messages in canisters clipped to the birds' legs. Finally, the agents released the pigeons, which flew home to England.

Top Secret

SPIES IN WORLD WAR II

By 1941, German troops had conquered most of western Europe. Hitler now planned to send an invasion force across the Channel to Britain. Could the work of spies help to stop him?

Resistance fighters attack a German barracks in France during World War II.

Into Occupied Territory

Thousands of Allied men and women slipped secretly behind enemy lines. Some agents were dropped by parachute, others landed from small boats or submarines. They infiltrated countries occupied by German troops, including France, Belgium, Greece, and Yugoslavia. Once in position, they gathered intelligence, organized local agents, and sent back information to Britain by radio, **courier**, or even by pigeon. They lived in constant danger of arrest, and many were caught and executed.

Defying the Enemy

The agents relied on the help and protection of local people. In turn, they gave support to groups of resistance fighters. These were vital to the war effort. They attacked important transport links, such as railway stations, dockyards and air bases. They also ambushed German troops and their actions slowed down German invasion preparations, and drew away troops from other areas. Resistance groups usually lived rough in remote areas, and depended on agents to organize air drops of arms, ammunition, and other supplies.

Top Secret

Essential equipment for an agent behind the lines.

They should have one of the following:

- Silver cigarette case
- Gold ring
- Silk stockings

These items have no practical value, but can be used as gifts to bribe police and other officials.

SPY FILE

Pearl Cornioley (1914–2008)

In 1943, during World War II, British spy Pearl Cornioley parachuted into France and controlled more than 2,000 resistance fighters and oversaw more than 800 attacks on railroad lines. Germany offered 1 million Francs for her capture.

Deceiving the Enemy

By 1944, the Allies were planning their own invasion—
the D-Day landings in France. But first they used clever
deceptions to make the Germans believe the landings would
be made further north. Fake weapons and vehicles were
assembled at English ports opposite Calais (including blow-
up rubber tanks and plywood artillery). German spies in
Britain were fed false information, which they relayed to
Germany. And radio messages about the northern invasion
were sent to military units which didn't exist. The operation
was a complete success.

A soldier puts the
finishing touches to
a dummy rubber tank
on the English coast,
near Dover.

Some secret weapons carried by WWII agents:
1. A propelling pencil gun that fired one bullet.
2. A finger ring with a tiny blade, for slashing tires
   on enemy vehicles.
3. A suicide pill, which would kill just 5 seconds
   after swallowing.

Top Secret

The Body on the Beach

In April 1943, the body of a British soldier was found on a Spanish beach. In his pockets were documents giving plans for an Allied invasion of Sardinia. A Nazi spy sent the information to Germany, and Hitler immediately reinforced his troops in Sardinia. But the documents were fake, and the body didn't belong to a soldier. The whole thing was an Allied trick aimed at diverting German attention from the real Allied invasion target—Sicily.

SPY FILE

David Strangeways
(1913–98)

Strangeways began his World War II career as a British soldier fighting in North Africa. But he soon showed a brilliant gift for deception. He became the army's Chief Deception Officer, and masterminded Operation Quicksilver in 1944. Using false radio signals and other tricks, he fooled the Germans about the real plan for the D-Day landings.

The body of this dead soldier, washed up on the Spanish coast, was planted with fake documents to mislead German agents.

SPYING IN THE COLD WAR

At the end of World War II, two **superpowers** dominated the world—the United States and the Soviet Union. The invention of the atomic bomb gave them the deadliest weapon in history.

Building the Bomb

The first bomb had been developed in the U.S., at Los Alamos in the New Mexico desert. Here, a team of Western scientists worked to split the atom. Naturally, they wanted to keep their findings secret—especially from their rival superpower. But the Soviets knew all about the project. Among the top brains at Los Alamos was a German, Klaus Fuchs, who passed vital information to the Soviet secret service. His work allowed the Soviet Union to build its own atomic bomb.

During the 1940s, scientist Klaus Fuchs leaked details of the West's atomic bomb to the Soviet Union.

Superpower Secret Services

The struggle between the United States and the Soviet Union was known as the "Cold War," because they never actually fought each other in battle. But each side fought intelligence battles, using spies as soldiers. These were run by their giant secret service organizations, which controlled vast networks of spies and spying equipment, and processed information. The Americans had the CIA (Central Intelligence Agency), while the Soviets had the KGB (Committee of State Security).

This is the emblem of the CIA. The Agency has collected, analyzed, and **evaluated** foreign intelligence for the United States since 1947.

SPY FILE

Francis Gary Powers (1929–77)

Powers was the pilot of an American U-2 spy plane. In May 1960, he was shot down while flying over the Soviet Union, photographing military bases. Following a lot of publicity and a **show trial**, the Russians imprisoned him for spying. Powers was released to the U.S. in 1962.

25

DOUBLE AGENTS

A double agent is someone who works in the secret service of one side, but who is actually spying for the other side.

Cold War Traitors

Double agents are in a perfect position to steal secrets and pass them to the enemy. However, they run a huge risk every day. The most famous double agents of the Cold War were known as the "Cambridge Spy Ring." Kim Philby, Donald Maclean, and two others met when they were students at Cambridge University, and went on to work for British intelligence services. But all of them were really Soviet spies who leaked important information to the Russians.

The Lubyanka is the popular name for the headquarters of the Federal Security Service (FSB) in Russia.

The Game's Up

When double agents are exposed, they have only one way out—to **defect**, or run away, to the country for which they are really spying. This happened many times during the Cold War. Two of the Cambridge Five fled to Russia in 1951, when they learned that MI5 suspected them. In 1985, Russian agent Oleg Gordievsky defected to Britain and wrote a bestselling book about his career. However, many double agents get caught. Robert Hanssen, an FBI agent, was arrested in 2001 after 20 years of selling secrets to Russia.

Former FBI agent Robert Hanssen (b. 1944) was a spy for the Russian KGB. He worked under the code name Ramon Garcia and delivered American state secrets in plastic trash bags. Unfortunately for Hanssen, he left his fingerprints on the bags and was caught.

SPY FILE

Oleg Penkovsky (1919-63)

Penkovsky was an officer in Soviet military intelligence. During a visit to London in 1961 he began passing information about Russian nuclear weapons to Western agents. He hoped this might prevent a war. He was arrested by Soviet police and executed.

SECRET WAR ON TERROR

The Cold War ended with the collapse of Communism in the early 1990s. But a new conflict quickly took its place—the war against world terrorism.

The Shock of 9/11

On September 11, 2001, terrorists **hijacked** four U.S. airliners. They flew two of them into the World Trade Center in New York, causing massive damage and 3,000 deaths. The terrorists belonged to militant **Islamic** groups, which had vowed to kill Americans and their allies. These terrible events took the Western world by surprise. U.S. intelligence agencies had failed to give any warning. They had no agents inside the Islamic terrorist movement, and could not intercept their messages.

The towers of the World Trade Center in New York both had 110 stories. They collapsed within two hours of the attacks.

Agents and al-Qaeda

Since 9/11, secret services around the world have had to develop some new spying techniques. Terrorist groups, such as **al-Qaeda**, are very difficult to penetrate, and double agents are rare. They seldom use radio contact, so their messages are hard to intercept. As a result, intelligence agencies have made use of new technology, such as CCTV cameras and satellite imaging. They have also tried to think ahead, by freezing the finances of terror groups, and keeping a close watch on new weapons, such as mass poisons and **radioactive bombs**.

SPY FILE

Omar Nasiri

(b.1960s)

Moroccan Nasiri (not his real name) joined an Islamic terror group in the 1990s, but soon grew alarmed by its goals. He began passing information to French and British intelligence services. Later, he even infiltrated an al-Qaeda training camp in Afghanistan.

Spy satellites circle the Earth, keeping watch on a variety of activities below. These satellites can spot objects as small as a cat and beam back electronic information to tracking stations in the U.S. and UK.

GLOSSARY

Allies a group of nations, including Britain, Russia, and the U.S., who were united against the "Axis" nations, led by Germany, in World War II

al–Qaeda an extreme Islamic terrorist organization which has carried out many violent acts, including the September 11, 2001, attack on New York

American Revolution the war (1775–81) in which the American colonies gained their independence from British rule

besiege to surround a city with an army in an attempt to capture it

bribery making someone act dishonestly by offering them money or some other payment

Confederacy the group of mainly southern states that joined together in 1860 to withdraw from the other United States. The Confederate Army was beaten by the Union Army in the Civil War

courier a messenger; someone who carries information from one person to another

deception tricking someone into believing something false

defect to desert or leave one's own country in order to join the enemy

evaluate to fix the value or worth of something

Geneva Convention an agreement (begun in 1864) between nations on the rules for the treatment of prisoners and the wounded in wartime

George Washington (1732-99) the general who led the colonial forces during the American Revolution. He later became the first president of the United States

hijack to take illegal control of an aircraft or other vehicle

infiltrate to gain entry to an organization or place in disguise or in secret, to find out secrets and pass them on

intelligence   useful or secret knowledge about the enemy collected by spies

intercept   to stop or seize something on its way to another destination

Islamic   belonging to Islam. Followers of the Islamic religion are called Muslims.

Mongols   the people of Mongolia, who built up a huge empire under Genghis Khan

papyrus   an early type of paper made from flattened reeds

pitched battle   a fierce fight between two armies in close contact

radioactive bomb   a bomb that explodes and scatters harmful radioactive material

recruit   to enlist or persuade someone to serve in a company or the armed forces

resistance fighter   a non-soldier who fights against an army occupying his or her country

sabotage   to damage or destroy equipment or buildings belonging to the enemy, especially in secret

show trial   a trial conducted mainly to make an impression of power on the public or on other nations

superpower   a very powerful nation which dominates its neighboring countries. Between 1945 and 1990, the two major world superpowers were the U.S. and the Soviet Union

U–boat   a German submarine in World War I or World War II

Union   the name given to the northern states who fought against the south, or Confederacy, in the American Civil War

volunteer   someone who joins an organization or gives help of his or her own free will

vulnerable   easily wounded or damaged

INDEX

WEB FINDER

http://www.coldwar.org
All aspects of the Cold War, with lots of information about espionage

https://www.cia.gov/library/publications/additional-publications/civil-war/
Spying during the American Civil War

http://www.spartacus.schoolnet.co.uk/FRresist.htm
Exciting details about French Resistance fighters of World War II

https://www.cia.gov/kids-page/games/break-the-code/index.html
Information about different codes plus some challenges to break-the-codes